City of Midnight Skies

POEMS ★ DRAWINGS

CITY OF MIDNIGHT SKIES

Stephen Gibson

HORSE & BUGGY PRESS

Raleigh, North Carolina FALL 2001

Thanks to the following publications
in which these works first appeared.

BOSTON REVIEW
Notes From An Apartment, Robert Desnos,
To Her, The Revival Of Patsy Montana

BROWNSTONE REVIEW
The Port Of Olympia

CHAIN
Arc Light, City of Rilke's Desire, Replicate the Years

DOUBLE NEGATIVE
Coasting

GARGOYLE
Last Blues

LEDGE
September

PHOEBE
Left On Her Machine

POETRY NORTHWEST
The Waiting, Disappearing By The Cape Fear,
The Erotic Dreams of The Poor, Late City

RAIN CITY REVIEW
Third Letter to M.

ULULATION
Southern Mountains

WASHINGTON REVIEW
First Letter to M.

WATCHWORD
Second Letter to M.

Published and Distributed by
Horse & Buggy Press
Antfarm Studios
303 Kinsey Street
Raleigh, North Carolina 27603
(919) 828–2514
horseandbuggypress@yahoo.com

FIRST EDITION

Covers and title pages were letterpress
printed on a hand-fed Vandercook SP–20
at the Horse & Buggy Press print shop.

Interior paper is New Leaf Opaque
70 lb text, a recycled paper which
was processed chlorine-free, meaning
no dioxins have been introduced into
the water system. This paper contains
60% post-consumer waste content
and is 80% overall recycled fiber.

New Leaf Opaque is distributed out
of San Francisco and New York City
offices by New Leaf Paper. For more
info, visit www.newleafpaper.com.

CONTENTS

I have always defended the skies of my youth.

Louis Aragon

SOMETIMES CITY FRAGMENTS

Sometimes I love walking out from my office into the middle of this city. I always want to be there for this hour when everything pauses, when the capsule breaks open and the evening's blue liquid begins to seep out, darkening everything as night comes on. I love this hour after rush hour, when the shadows lengthen beneath parked cars, and the empty buildings seem to raise themselves floor by fluorescent floor over the darkening world below them. At these times I feel thoughtful but empty, tired from the day's work, happy just to notice the airplanes lowering themselves over the river and to smell the wind blowing through the air.

Sometimes I want the world to teach me how to understand things. Sometimes I just want to rub the static into my eyes as the traffic falls endlessly down 19th Street like a grand procession of headlights going nowhere through the occasion of the dusk. And there they are mouthing words into cell phones as their cars float through red signals at intersections. And who is to say that they aren't simply distracted by their own dreaming? Even if they are dreaming of something so commonplace that they will actually be able to reach out and touch it at the end of their terrible commute to the suburbs, while we will remain standing on these sidewalks long after they are gone, nearly devoured by the bitterness of our own lofty dreaming?

And you would think that some of these things were treasures. That some of these things were treasured. The broken umbrellas littering the streets after each storm like the skeletons of some extinct variety of flightless bird. The little hot-dog stands being towed into the evening. The cops driving around almost inconspicuously in their unmarked cars, searching everywhere for something wrong. That man selling flowers from a dry wall bucket by the subway entrance, the German tourists in the bookstore, those women marching down K Street in those long black skirts slit up the back, all of these things become the world.

Who can touch the singing inside their own body? Who can look at a face and fall in love? Sometimes I wonder which part of the jewel I will touch, which part I will hide under my shirt and make promises to and cry for when it outgrows me?

Sometimes the soft sound of the traffic of cars out the window when I come home late and close the door sounds like rain falling in the tunnels of sleep. Swish and brush of headlights tracing shadows diagonally across my walls and ceiling, as if across the tiled walls of a tunnel below a harbor, where gray battleships are sliding out in the night, to disappear at sea....

What you have been watching and what you have been dreaming are the false pretensions of the planet's wealthiest men, burning forests down, floating their hydroplanes across the Everglades of Cash. So what. Tonight there is a summer thunderstorm watch in effect although it is so hot out I don't believe it will rain for days. I look out the window to the north and see the sky spreading out for the evening, the pinks and oranges and blues of a beautiful pollution. I lie down on the couch and reach for a book. What would Rilke say to us now, here at the end of this century of loneliness that he began? What would he say from his room in some rich Lady's castle, after the World Wars and the Cold War, now that the triumph of the First World of the Heart is complete?

In time, the great secrets will be revealed. The mysteries of our bodies floating through these sequences of star light will fall away, revealing the faces of the people we meant to become. Certain city states will rise or fall in prominence. Lord Stanley's Cup will change hands. Lovers be re-united, Pretenders to the throne and their confederates returned to the rough deserts from which they came…

Yes, one day we will all escape. The dark water towers poised so long for lift off will finally reveal themselves as the escape rockets we long dreamed they might become. The river will rise, flooding the jogging paths, and the traffic of satellites orbiting our planet will become more beautiful to us than the stars. Only a hush will remain. For a moment it will contain everything like a thought or a breath held in expectation. And it will sound like the strange silence of crowded elevators. The silence of fathers. Silence of the sky over the wind.

Monday morning was routine. Doc was at

the bar. Wall Street was doing fine.   Doc drank six bourbons and forgot about

everything his shrink had insisted   he remember. "I remember...."

THE EMBARCADERO

Those tugboats
Pushing construction barges over the green waters of the bay
Aren't sure if they are moving through a joy
Or a loneliness and I'm not sure
I can help them understand the difference.
Across the water beyond this
Treasure Island and the traffic sliding and jamming
On the bridge overhead the Oakland hills
Cower in the distance.
Today is clear summer perfection and the sky
Is wide and silent
And our hearts are wrecked.
I'm like everyone else sitting here along the Embarcadero
Eating a sandwich and drinking Coke from a waxed-paper cup
With my tie flipped over one shoulder and my eyes
Shrinking behind my sunglasses.
I drink and drink until there is only ice
But I do not rise when I am finished
And go back to work.
I keep sitting here waiting for the sunlight to fade
And change the way
The water looks.
I'm going to wait for this sunlight to turn into the darkness
That separates our days from our dreams.

THE WAITING

We watch these men pull out of their underground
Garages and punch the steering wheels
When lights go red before them and they are
Furious with this
Delay believing that their law firm or insurance
Agency or government
Should move them unconditionally
Through the evening crowd of people like us
Who stand under the awnings of used bookstores
To keep out of the rain in this first hour of neon
As it reflects across the covers of books
And magazines while offices empty and windows begin
Explaining how they color our eyes with what's not there
Like these ugly expensive women's shoes or travel
Posters insinuating what fun we should be enjoying in
The thinly lacquered grandeur of tropical beaches very
Very far from here where we stare in expectation of a
Silence that will arrive like Independence over
These flagpoles and rooftop ventilators
And our upwards pointed faces at rush hour's end
When the thinking clouds come on bringing with them
The real darkness which is our own

PHOTOGRAPHS OF TELEVISIONS IN HOTEL ROOMS

The narrative age is over, now
There's just a series of images smeared by rain
And evening light, and the reflections of headlights
That slide across the tiles.
I hang-up the phone and then push out of the office,
Snapping my umbrella open as I hit the sidewalk,
Then hold it over my head like a sad thought.
As I walk up 19th Street I see my friend
Waiting outside the coffee shop,
Then follow her inside.
On the walls it's the usual postmodern iconography—
Star Trek crap and Elvis shit,
And photographs of televisions in hotel rooms.
Pictures of couches and empty chairs
Lit by ugly light.
I watch my friend lift a ten dollar bill
From her small wallet
As they hiss her steaming milk.
O Captain Elvis, with your blue suede shoes
And lonely combed-up pompadour,
Help me remember now
What I meant to do with my life!
I grab the drink from the counter and turn around,
Walking back toward the door through the din
And smoky conversation,
Part of the echoing nothingness
Responding with its unpopular response.
We stand outside because the rain has stopped,
Watching the traffic inch around DuPont Circle,
Holding our coffees with both hands to keep warm.
She points to the broken clock over the bank next door,
Wondering out loud how long it has been stuck
In that used-up hour,
Or if it's just waiting like that in expectation of
The significant hour to come?

ROBERT DESNOS

I am going to dedicate my life to the writing of
Surreal poems of love
But I will not talk to anyone about it except you
I will walk down to the cafe and listen to the table wood
I will reach through these shields of the night forever
Finding only your name where it lingers
With the last leaves on trees at the edge of a park
A park creating emptiness and oblivion with its white sky
Simply that I may trace
My dark path under it
This is the world domination of loneliness
This is a red wine nightmare through which I drive
Mountain roads endlessly toward the rumor
Of the idea of you this is the silence
Carrying out my orders and these
Are your words drifting from my mouth like smoke
Up into the vast constellations of stars
That mirror the pain and consolation inside our own bodies
Sometimes I put my hands in my pockets
As if they were reaching for a shyness but when they close
The bedroom door they only want to call to you
Through the megaphone of this pillow
And begin the search for you
Through these dreams

THE EROTIC DREAMS OF THE POOR

If you were here I'd like to lie here touching you
In this darkness my voice against your skin teaching
The soft pages nobody explains the soft pages
Of rain delivered across the avenues and yet
I'd find your mouth as if I were returning to the years
Of salt to those cities of grief in our air
So that reaching out to hold them their shimmering
Would become our transfer from this moment to another
One of interiors growing dark growing specific like
When we stick a candle in a bottle and call that
A winter night while listening to this tape of a woman
Singing to us about romance and disappearance
Airport access roads and the grand coasts of betrayal
To our south from which we return and care nothing
For only this darkness around us like hair thrown down
Across our faces while we kiss and I whisper It's alright
I know the rich go on with their own special laws
That they lift silver to their lips with meat-shaped forks
Because I have wandered their streets in my bad tuxedo
Searching for your everywhere and come only to this river
With its skin of oil as colorful as sleep might seem
After many nights alone with you

DISAPPEARING BY THE CAPE FEAR

That night we drank beer from cans on the balcony
Of this two-story motel and of course there was neon
Reflecting up from the wet streets of the off season
From restaurants and clubs and the docked boats
That swayed like shadows in the harbor by McDonald's
And she and I had our legs up on the railing touching
When the lighthouse lights became apparent
Sweeping across the inlet waters during those
The last few moments we had left of sunset
And then the stars came out so quickly it was almost
As if their meanings would get lost inside our bodies
Like those dark barges on the night river that were
Gone when morning came to us from outside our room's
Thick curtains and we never spoke of that silence
Again not even to each other on the road

TO HER

I thought you'd like to be a sailor on a ship gone out to sea
I thought you'd been a sailor
Or that you lived in some western town ranged with mountains
One main street running through it
Like places I've seen in South Dakota or Montana
And I imagined how nice it would be to live there
I have wanted to be able to touch your life sometimes
And the details of your routine
But so you couldn't see me
Or my campfire hidden against the hills
You might recognize my rain falling in valleys to the south
And the warm white ashes in your stove
But inside yourself you'd feel nothing except the grass and air
And that would be alright
Sometimes I have wanted to write to you
About solitude
And loneliness and their imitators
These long black shadows
That spoke out from around glowing street lamps
I have wanted to say something to you about the past
That's gone and
Something about the past that stays
And never quits its wanting
And I have pictured myself writing this letter
Alone in some room
Typing to you over a city of rooftops
Where electric light never obscures the stars
But already it is May and even at night
Too hot to wear a shirt at home too hot to wear my watch
Sometimes then I find myself downtown drinking in bars
Where men curse their girlfriends as sexy music
Blares from the jukebox and while I know sadness
Is never an excuse sometimes I swear
They say a word and they might as well have touched you

LEFT ON HER MACHINE

The snow has turned tonight to rain,
And the streets are bright with it.
There are freighters sliding out into nothing
And you can't see them as they turn
For an ocean miles from here.
Last summer, from Hurricane Ridge we saw
The Strait of Juan de Fuca, and the winking silver
Shipping there. Those diamonds between Canada
And our small lives were smiling, and we kept quiet
For some time, so they could know us.

And there are red lights on roofs
Across this city, opening
And closing, and I can feel that way
Without you.
I walked down Broadway an hour ago, slowly
And totally without purpose. Is it winter now
That the last leaves have broken
For the fences? You told me that it was.

My coat's on the chair by the window
With the shade down. And I wonder if you can leave
The world without actually dying? Maybe
If I drove south through Oregon,
Wrote you postcards from places I have never been.
After ten hours sleep I could pull my boots on
And stare at motel carpet with the radio on low.

I am looking at a map and wondering what a life
Costs. What it takes to get to the "what"
Of what it's worth. The trees outside are black
As the dots that stand for ruined towns
Between rivers. There are lines on this map that don't
Mean anything at all.

LATE CITY

Yes it is always late in this city
Shirts hang encased in plastic
On mechanical lines in the cleaner's windows
And parking garages have emptied so that the oil stained
Concrete changes into the geography of something
Unnecessary and unused something that can give
It's full face to the moon
Like a school playground just covered with snow
No one has broken a path across yet
Inside bars and taverns the chairs are on the tables
The fire station doors are shut and no Dalmatian
Sits outside pricking its ears at passing cars
There never was a Dalmatian
There never was an old woman asking for help across the street
There never were flowers on the First of May or a happiness
In the ideological hearts of our fathers
But there are these shopping carts pushed one
Inside the other beside the whispering
Automatic doors of the 24 hour supermarket
Where the gas station attendant stirs his coffee and talks to
A clerk while others are stocking shelves
Watering produce or cutting down cardboard boxes with
Their razor blades
It's almost a form of privacy this moving through the night
Here at the end of a century of
Solitude and speed
You might even find the city is not ugly without people
The statues continue saluting the skies
And the paint on houses keeps on being paint
And looking across the river there will always be
The smeared lights of cars coursing along the parkways
Moving smoothly through the darkness towards
Something none of us has seen

CITY of RILKE'S DESIRE

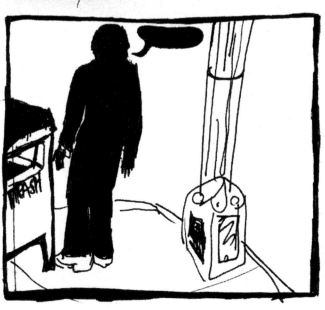

HEDONISM

We cash our checks at the Galaxy Liquor Store, spend some of that
new money right there, then go back to the company office and drink
some more with our dispatcher. It's his birthday and everyone is having
a good time. Now Marcus has got it in his mind to ride up Mount
Pleasant Street and buy some of that "sweet shit." He rides ahead of me
on his bicycle, so when I catch up to him at the dark corner of a side
street, he is already sitting down on the curb between the men with the
folding chairs who seem to own this intersection and signal to everyone
who passes by. Conversation, vague transactions ensue. Because I am
with Marcus, everyone shakes my hand and delivers the punch lines
of their jokes in my direction, so I can laugh with them. This is not
Rilke in Paris. This is Washington, D.C. in August, so when my friend
has got his shit, or made arrangements to pick it up, I say "See you
later," and leave him to the next stage of his night. I turn toward
the possibility of the Black Cat. Always the promise that some of the
fellas might already be standing at the bar with their backs to the world.
And now the sky is clear following this afternoon's brief rain and it is
good to see how the clouds coasting in on such a glorious high pressure
system can hint at the autumn weather to come. I can't help but look
up as I pedal. I like the way those clouds glide in over the skyline, like
kings in a procession. Self-confident, not searching for anything.

FIRST LETTER TO M.

What I do here in D.C. is I ride my bicycle as a messenger all day and when I come home from work I'm tired and angry. I'm still young enough to half believe most of this anger is just stored energy and sometimes you need it that way when you have to kick the cab that changes lanes into you at DuPont Circle. Sometimes you want to smash his rear view mirror saying "You won't be needing that anymore Motherfucker" and continue riding as hard as your heart and legs and lungs will move you through the rush hour. I get home and eat something then sit at the kitchen window and think about that white space that surrounds us when we sleep. That you might feel when you sit at the edge of your bed loading and unloading a snub nose .38 or that you might also have felt while riding a ferry across a northern Sound. This is the feeling I concentrate on. Tonight, one of those summer thunderstorms is approaching, flashing its dry lightning across the parkway, sort of a hazy reflection of the psychic landscape I traveled through earlier that is only now breaking out into this shared atmosphere. The rain won't begin until well after dark.

In the mornings my writing tends to make some sense. At night I am just too tired and spaced out, like tonight, if I wrote to you I would begin with the same old shit, that one poem in which I watch people hurrying through bus exhaust to greet their lives of ash. The one about courtrooms and hallways in postmodern office buildings where my image is frozen in video surveillance cameras for a few gray seconds. The one where aircraft descend across the river of my heart! Where clouds wheel in over the empty parking lots of this swamp where they built our Nation's Capital, the city where I was born, and she has left me once again…

I could go on. Of course my friend, Matt Redd, the cowboy I have spoken of from Utah fell into my life a couple of days ago, unexpected and unannounced as usual. He tells me about the bear he and the foreman from his ranch caught and let loose in a bar near Colorado. How Fish & Wildlife weren't amused. He says he's sent some books that I should get after he is gone and asks me what new jokes I know.

His last night here I took him down to the Black Cat and around the corner to another more expensive place, then back to the faithful Gato Negra, and as we were walking there around 14th and U I got that good city feeling again for the first time in a long while. All the crap I overlook during work every day existed that night in its true moment of perfection: that old man mumbling outside the pharmacy looked almost distinguished holding his coat together, cane hooked over one arm. The smiling advertisements and tawdry awnings beamed with meaning beyond their graffiti and we felt the buoyant summer air brush through the trees to come down and walk with us, no, to move us along streets past all the strip joints and bars and restaurants with their doors and windows open. Even the dark lot of the used car place looked austere but magnificent, fenced in with its tinsel and colored pennants and razor wire.

Nights like that are where I used to draw my ammunition from, but I'm too tired to work much into poems. I'm just the shithead writing pretty letters now. I used to imagine that if I could make myself healthy and smart then I would feel content in life with the golden promise of my soul. Poor, schmoore, I thought. But each night my teeth inch closer to an expensive surgery I will never be able to afford, and I feel uncomfortable sometimes when I run into old friends from the punk rock days, who have graduated from law school. But I have felt that white space move in over aerials and satellite dishes of rooftops downtown, and it has cooled me at the end of the day as I rode home, passing my reflection across glass storefronts and the trees all humming with the first green buds of the season. Tonight I watch the slow barges move across the river I can see from my window between the steam plant and those warehouses. Soon the rain will start. The beer bottle sweats, the knife lies next to the bread. Sometimes I relax enough to feel the weight of the things I touch evening after evening, and I feel slightly less discouraged if it has taken me an entire year to write a single poem I don't hate at the end of the month. But isn't this the lesson Rilke taught us? That it might take my life.

SECOND LETTER TO M.

Like what you said about my job as a bicycle messenger, Isn't that
beautiful. You said, Isn't that beautiful, how I might walk into a room
and deliver the words that could change someone's life! Well. More
often it feels like what I'm delivering is cellular phones left behind
at cross town staff meetings or Congressional press releases that go to
magazines with names like *Defense Complex Monitor* or *Radiation Week*.
Almost daily I take passports from Coca-Cola for authentication at
the embassies of developing nations up and down Massachusetts
Avenue. But I like it sometimes. Leaning over to unlock my bicycle
from a street sign or a parking meter at the end of the day, the anger
that grew within me all afternoon can simply disappear—and it feels
good to be there with that slight city breeze brushing across my face
as the traffic rushes up 15th Street behind me. I've got the key in my
hand, the U-lock in my pocket, my bike between my legs: and I watch
the shelves and honeycombs of light begin to shine from the very same
buildings that rose so stupidly over the lunch hour. Sometimes I can
believe that they might shine for me alone.

And then I'm riding home, maneuvering down streets that slide like
tunnels through the skyline's dirty glaciers. I'm doing errands. And of
course it is in one of those enormous drug stores in which you get
lost in the aisles without remembering what you came in looking for,
and in which I could never imagine anyone coming to fill a prescrip-
tion, there being just too much of everything no one needs here.
But the advertisements in the large windows were offering me back
my life, recommending Sale Items! and there was one thing I needed.
So I wander the bright aisles, the floors seemingly the source of this
overall fluorescence illuminating the walls and ceilings, walking around
like an astronaut in space, until I eventually find the pomade and the
condoms and the fruit-punch flavored Gatorade I came in for. But
those little red vests the check out clerks have to wear make me so
sad. One clerk waves my items across the glass part of the counter
a few times until we hear the beep of each price registering, and then
she places them in a white plastic sack. I hate it. But it's too late to
say, Look, that's alright, I have my own bag, so I take the little sack
from her hand and walk outside.

THIRD LETTER TO M.

I'm still here in an eastern city that smells like piss in the night, and sometimes I forget that this moment turns the wheels of stars invisible above us. There are no mountains here, but you knew that, only the dull marble of these monuments you might extend a hand to and touch the names of those our country lost. And they are all here. Washington, D.C. in the insufferable summer with its slaughtering mist hanging low over the mighty Potomac, revealing it for what it has become: just a little stream shadowing under its bridges. And tonight I might make my way down to the Black Cat, wait for Johnny the Boy to show up and watch the hip kids lean across the bar picking lint from dollar bills as they order micro brews and mixed drinks. But sometimes I get so sick of myself for sitting there listening to the same crappy Social Distortion songs churn from the jukebox. Outside 14th Street answers with the silent lights and accelerating engine of a detective's unmarked car as it disembarks from a nearby convenience store for the yellow glare of the crime scene tape. Or, I'll ignore my heart when it says, Let's take a ride, a very, very long ride, and never return again to this humidity. We know the streets out there. That sad roulette of iron railings and trashed row houses. Faces illuminated in the green windows of buses passing by like traitors through a sleep that isn't theirs. And the pink marble of the empty Municipal Center that aches like something at the bottom of an arctic sea while clouds turn in from the suburbs, to awaken the evening in all of us.

Or I remember Seattle: those trains that run back and forth between the Boeing plant and the waterfront, flat cars stacked with containers and airplane wings and I couldn't even say exactly what, but I have watched that power roll through the empty midnight industrial district below Interstate 5. Six huge engines and all that freight. I watched that once when I was fucked up at some artist's party held in a warehouse out there in a neighborhood where nobody lived at all. I remember I went outside alone and watched the streetlights change over the desolate intersections and the slatted fences and the pieces of glass that seemed strewn about with such faith in themselves—and there I was waiting for my identity to walk out of the disguise of the world! every now and then a tow truck hissing through the mist behind me, and always that slight rain that you forget about.

But it's like what my friend, Dee, says about racing bicycles, about that
point in every race when you are hurting so bad that you have to
dig deep inside yourself, not just looking to how much pasta you ate
for dinner the night before or anything so simple, it's about reaching
further and longer and harder than maybe you ever have before. I listen
to him talking, and I understand what he is saying. Points in my life
have felt like that. I look back when it feels bad and I see journeys
I have taken and enjoyed that seem now like I was reaching for some-
thing I maybe never wanted to find. Then, suddenly, it was touching
against me, it was all around me, sharing its warmth as if it were an
animal or a lover. It was the world. I see myself standing over steaming
pine needles, pissing beside a logging road in the Cascades at night,
close to winter. With Jana playing pinball in a tavern in Olympia,
Washington. In her apartment there—the blue curtains blowing in
over us as we lie down together listening to an old Rolling Stones tape.
The powerlines we look at from her window, that follow one edge of
the equipment yards at the bottom of the Puget Sound, the powerlines
that she made a painting of. I see its reds and yellows now, and the
black car in it too. For awhile those seemed like the only moments,
but I should know they continue to arrive especially when I am too
preoccupied to care. Like last Sunday, watching the bike races down-
town, Dee and I were yelling "Move up, Zach!" to our friend who
was racing. "Move up, Zach!" every time the peloton turned the corner
already going fast as shit, whirrring past us right there by the Securities
and Exchange Commission where we deliver packages every working
day, as we drank beer in its shade and laughed during this, the final race
of the afternoon. Dee and me shouting "Move up, Zach!" and laughing
in the shade.

NICKY

In my experience from going out into bars and nightclubs I can tell
you there is always some fucker named "Nicky" around. While I am
at home going through the pages of the Victoria's Secret catalogue I
stole from my neighbor's mailbox, he is watching his beautiful girlfriend
cook dinner for him. When I am sitting at the bar in the hour before
people actually go out to that bar, he is tying his shoes after making
love for hours. Just when I think I have said something funny to
the bartender the bartender looks the other way and shouts "Nicky!"
as Nicky walks in and it's as if I had never said a word to anyone in
the world since the fifth grade when I was a King.

COASTING

Tonight, riding home, I keep looking up at the distant radio towers, and watching the red lights flash on and off over the city and the hills. As I ride, the summer night is just beginning around me. And I like it, this overlapping hour between coming home and going out, the hour of cars circling the blocks in search of parking, of laughter from rooftop restaurants, and music that echoes into the street from open bar room doors. Downtown, people are still walking to their subway stops, while behind them the internally lit office buildings are becoming palaces—block after block of burning light simmering toward a brown-out. I ride hard through traffic, noticing turn signals, smelling the pollen in the air, and wondering to myself what is important in this world? At this moment someone I know might be lifting money from their wallet at a crowded happy hour, or staring at closed storefronts filled with fashion magazines and other attention getting devices. I am seeking to find the meaning below the static of the merchandise. Then, at the top of the rise, I stop pedaling and let myself coast down the last avenue. Overhead, the sequences click on. Click off. I can see the sunset like a forest fire slow-walking across the suburbs beyond the river, heading west. "Touch me now, in this fading light…" might be words to a song I would like to hear right now, or they might be the words I want to say to you when we are lying together in the darkness, and the night is cool across the city once again. Click on, and I am coming. Click off, I'm almost there.

IN THE SOUTHEASTERN NIGHT

Last night there was an eclipse of the moon, did you see it? I asked
my friend today what came between the moon and us and she said
no. We came between the sun and the moon. And I had seen our
shadow track across the whiteness making it seem smoky. Hazy. Close.
It was gray at first then at last the blackness of the eclipse—our shadow—
was just a little hat cocked diagonally on top of the moon's head.
And as I watched this I was listening to old honky-tonk music. Ray
Price. Some George Jones. And I drank beer by the window watching
the sky and listening to the tinkling piano, that brittle sounding
brilliance of a time gone by. The pedal steel guitar and the chug-chug
fiddle intros and the voices of the cool singers yelling out their
loneliness and yearning to the sweaty, broken-hearted crowds saying,
It's alright to feel this sad. It's alright to feel this way, America, you
know we have before. And from now on.

ELECTRIC SNOWFLAKE SHAPED LIGHTS
ON CONNECTICUT AVENUE

It's almost Thanksgiving and that run of the holiday season again which means that all of the New York people will be showing up in town with their flared black pants and expensive haircuts. I already know they'll want to go out to places like the 18th Street Lounge every night they are here. They'll want to smoke cigars and order drinks with names that New York will have forgotten by the time the bartenders down here figure out what combination of juice and liquor and coloring to pour into what type of glass. But maybe not. I was downtown this evening and noticed that the first Christmas decorations have been positioned on the street lamps up and down Connecticut Avenue. I think they look so good in the early darkness when the sidewalks are full of people hurrying between buildings and the streets are full of cars. It's the usual congestion bustling by but for a few weeks at least it will be illuminated by lights that suggest festivity and holiness and shopping. The stores are all decked out with appliances and bright coats and sweaters situated in the landscape of an artificial foil like snow. Some of the display windows even have prices written across them in shaving cream or something that's supposed to be snow too. Cartoon captions bubbling from the mouths of top-hatted snow men. That sort of thing. Sometimes there is almost the look of snow in all that fake snow. But never that type of silence.

THE FOUR SEASONS

In the evening heat rises from the ground up into the cooling air. This
is when dogs in the park catch a scent and want to run as if they were
still supposed to hunt. And we sense something about this time of day
as well. Things around us achieve a certain clarity and hidden instincts
we thought were lost return to us. For example I have seen the shapes
of buildings through the windows of other buildings but had no words
to describe what I needed to do. It is October. This afternoon the high
pressure system moving south from Canada put so many white clouds
across the sky it looked like the skies in oil paintings from a previous
century. October with your vegetables and sad leaves and tunnels of
golden light what are we to do with this? Mundane city things happen.
Trucks charge out of alleys. Construction on the new arena continues.
Couriers come and go from the offices. Sometimes there are the
smells of coffee or of wood smoke from a restaurant and then it's night.
I know the ghost light of stars tries to reach out to us in our cities
but it is no longer glamorous or illicit enough to impress. Therefore
we spend our lives looking for something to replace it with. Our bodies
want to walk beneath swimming galaxies and feel cold and search for
wood to burn on a damp night but instead we drive home past the
dozens of limousines and their police escorts idling in front of a luxury
hotel. The cops in their riding breeches smoke cigars and bullshit
with the limo drivers. Flags of whatever countries or corporations
hang folded over the miniature staffs while the cars stand still. There is
a clock overhead and it goes on telling the time. There is a river a few
blocks away damaged yes but still following its old course to the sea.
The traffic flows by. Sometimes more sometimes less. For now the
sirens and lights remain quiet and still hidden behind the grills of the
unmarked cars. There is no danger.

I CAN SEE THE MACHINERY TURNING
BEHIND THE DRYWALL, EVEN NOW

I think I saw the guy you call Mr. Roboto last week near DuPont
Circle, but he had his back to me, so I couldn't be sure. He was about
my height, same color hair, same black coat buttoned up over a black
suit, but when he turned around a cloud passed over the street, and
his face went dark. The wind blew hard for a minute, and plastic bags
from the hot dog stand rose into the air and snagged in the branches
of a tree beside my office building. Then, the sun came back out, and
the shadows seemed to shift like the teeth of a gear that was turning,
until the world relaxed the strength of its grip and brightened again
in the unfading of the moment. I crossed the street to find him, but
he was gone.

You have said that part of his face is always pointed to the sky, but
that his heart is as heavy as the lead boots the deep-sea diver wears
at the bottom of your old aquarium. But, I think I can understand
his loneliness, how it's possible to feel like a machine shaped like
a man, or a man who is turning into a robot. When he walks to work,
he follows the lines on the sidewalk. When he drives, he waits for
the lights. His days are filled with sequences of numbers, strings of
unlike words joined together. These are the codes he must keep secret.
And I'm sure he has a magnetic building pass, just like mine, only
I bet his can take him to the highest floors, and get him deeper below
the surface, probably even to a level below the vaults. He knows about
encryption.

Mr. Roboto held the door open for me this morning, but I felt his
thoughts were elsewhere. Inside of him, girls I know were acting shy
at parties, catching his attention, and then laughing to each other as
they turned their faces away. Inside of him metal rods rose and fell,
as if a key had been turned within the body of a lock. Snow was
falling on the carcass of a deer, dead beside the highway, and music
was coming from the back porch, as he opened the screen door to
walk out into the lime grove. I could see him turning off his flash light
as he headed down the fire road alone. When he comes back, it will
be with an armful of those flowers that open only in the moonlight,
and the party will be over.

REPLICATE THE YEARS

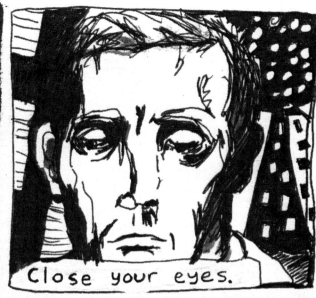

Close your eyes.

We are going to replicate

the years. Remember us perhaps if you will in your dreams...

NOTES FROM AN APARTMENT

I go outside and stand on the concrete stairwell and watch
The city come on and brighten as the sun goes down
It is the moment when everything—the natural
And the electric are balanced and seem equal and now
That moment is fading
And what am I gripping this railing waiting for
The rain's soft congratulations?
Tell me I am not alone
Remind me that there are many levels of consciousness
And this is why the branches of trees sway
And touch over the canals in these April winds and why
Friday night flashes its arcade of lights like somebody
Opening their shirt on stage
And why I love it when those airplanes hurry
Small waves over the river behind the rain
They lower themselves to land so carefully
I can't deny that
But this is not everything!
Where is the majesty promised to me in my youth
By the world?
How far behind the easy resolution of television
And its perfect fingers handling cleaning products
Is the mystery
That I must put my coat on and walk downtown to study
The backs of those buildings recently exposed
By the tearing down and hauling away of their neighbors?
Why should I go down there and look up
At windowless walls painted black
Or at the rusty streaks where a staircase used to rise
Floor by floor toward the sky
And expect to find it there?

THE PORT OF OLYMPIA

Soft pillows of neon go down the rainy avenues tonight
Sometimes you can see stars alive in rain for seconds
Running the length of your car windshield in the station
Sometimes you can hear that hit song by Alice in Chains
Played repeatedly on the jukebox at McCoy's Tavern
When they leave the back door open to the parking lot

You fold the cuffs of your jacket and comb your hair
Nervously in the doorways of card rooms and diners
Because you don't smoke when it rains like the other men

You stare at the candelabra shape painted over the pawn shop
Across the street a long time or whatever shape that is
In this light and this rain the goods for sale look molten
The bicycle and chain saws and camouflage jumpsuits
Seem to shift to the left the outboard motor
Has a mouth that keeps moving

Beyond these streets sometimes you walk the equipment yards
Where prehistoric looking timber industry trucks are parked
Sometimes the piled limber looks hurt and orange
But it glows quietly to itself on gray evenings
Like this one and the next one and the one inside your hand

AFTERWORLD

You have opened your mouth and tasted the dark chimneys of bitterness
But don't be distressed.
You've done so much since you lay down on that bathroom floor
And floated away from us in your twenty-sixth year.
Here, now, the acorns have started falling from high trees
In the parks downtown and wet leaves are
Plastered to the sidewalks,
Black mouths that still want you to answer them.
There is my memory of you walking around
Like a ghost with a cowboy hat on, past the closed strip-joints,
Into shitty bars, of you swimming in the post-hurricane sea...
And on clear nights, there is also the vicious white breath
Of stars, anchored in the night by their silence.
How many miles of that did you pass through, traveling on your back
Through the sky?
Always in my life it seems there have been people so far from me
That I could never find them,
But since you are gone it turns out
That I can find you everywhere—
In your girlfriend's kiss.
In the cold metallic taste of beer from this can.
Even in the city skyline that shrinks on autumn evenings
So that it appears to become just a little diorama
Lit by imaginary lights.
And what do I have to say that I consider so important
That I am writing to someone who will never truly re-appear?
That by saying this, it is happening, that by saying this
You are listening?

   —for John Neff (1971-1997)

REACHING ACROSS THE SILENCE

Sometimes I want to feel private
and quiet and hidden
like a thought.
Like a tattoo on my hip I don't show anyone.
Like the getaway car keys stashed inside
a jar of pennies.
How can I say this?
There is your life of errands and e-mails
and grocery shopping after work,
but there is another life walking
beside you like a shadow.
It registers the coded flashings of a window
at sunset
and never tells you what it means.
I want to walk into that room, tear open the envelope,
and find out.
Once, there was a sequin
glittering on the shoulder of a rich woman's dress.
I looked into her eyes and they said nothing.

FALLING MAN

In one dream, I open the door
after work, and walk inside.
There is my reading chair, solid
in the corner, a couch,
built-in shelves lined with books
about the Civil War, photographs,
paintings and art work by friends on the walls...
I step inside, but I don't
turn on the light.
I shut the door, then lie face down
on the carpet,
winter coat all buttoned up, the galoshes
still covering my shoes.
It's almost eight o'clock and the heater hisses out
a generous helping of evening heat,
while outside people are stepping
down from buses, cement trucks
beep in reverse as they back out of mid-city
construction sites,
and men in suits like mine stride past cubicles
gripping the handles of brief cases,
just as I'm doing now.
It's a dream
so I try to open my eyes, but I can't
because I'm wondering about the
heaviness, about the burden
of a life of things.

THIS MORNING

I saw a turtle covered in mud
crossing the canal tow-path, big as my torso,
slow as time.
I saw three crows pecking at a dead snake in the road.
They didn't move when cars came close.
I surprised a great heron by the drain pipe
and saw the big carp he was waiting for
hovering like a white face below
the shadow of the water,
and another heron, later, across the river.
He was already flying.
Down the trail I came upon a smaller turtle
with fire-colored stripes on its shell.
It was the kind of turtle you could put in a shoe box
and take to school for a week,
and then I saw seven deer bounding through the woods
away from me like ghosts,
white tails raised with their ticks riding them
through the stillness of the brush.
There was a breeze after this and last night's rain
blew off the leaves
so that it sounded like rain once again in the cut.
I heard the sound of trucks
and distant mowing
and the rain blowing off of the leaves.

SOUTHERN MOUNTAINS

Somewhere beyond the years, beyond the night time ghost line
Of trees beside the highway,
I see the long-lined poems I want to write about Virginia,
About these mountains that once hid Jackson's army,
And long drives south at the end of the summer.
In the evenings, as the miles go by, the world can look so calm
But also full of longing in its silence.
By the end of August the leaves on all the trees
Have blown in the wind for so many months.
Wouldn't they just love to let go
And float away?

In seven or eight hours I will be in North Carolina drinking
Beer and listening to Steve Earle tapes on Hoss's porch,
His greasy dogs licking themselves under the table,
As lightning breaks across the Iron Mountains.
And later, I will sleep in a spare room
With heavy quilts pulled over against the chilly
Mountain air. In the morning
I will wake to the sound of the wind in the trees.
I'll open my eyes and see my bag on the floor, my boots
Shoved back against the wall,
And this post card you wrote from Memphis
Tacked beside the mirror.
Wondering how you are—I am here, hello.

THE STARS

And when you step out of the building you look up at the stars again
For the first time in a long time, and it seems
Like they are shining from some vast, detached silence
Just for you.
You feel alone for a minute,
But when you look back down you're still standing on K Street with
Dumb-ass cabs honking at each other and sirens converging
Then separating in the distance.
You button, then unbutton your jacket, and stare into the window
Of the new Bombay India restaurant.
One of the waiters moves from table to table, not looking
At the dining couples, lighting each white candle
Before things get too busy.
All you want to do is stand here, even with people all around you
Watching the fires come on,
Until a woman brushes by so closely
You can smell the shampoo in her hair and it smells
Like artificial strawberry or cherry Coke. You turn
To watch her rushing down the street before she disappears
Around the corner—trench coat
Belted over skirt-suit, running shoes and
Walkman on, tuned-in
To one of the radio stations of the earth,
Broadcasting to her solitude.

SEPTEMBER

It is September now
And still so much like August, except for the new way the light
slants down on the playground equipment in the park this evening,
And the idea that all those leaves
whispering to you in the breeze
Will soon begin changing colors before
disappearing altogether—
Blown away or simply absorbed by the wet darkness
Of the gutters and the streets.
For some it is good to think of the coming cool weather.
Of suede jackets and coffee
Flavored with chicory.
But for others walking across the bridge from DuPont Circle
Or watching their dogs running around the soccer fields
There is the sadness of another year
Winding down without them, and still they have come no closer
To finding their perfect job or that lover
Who understands them better than anyone else in the world.
But nothing tonight isn't calm.
Nothing doesn't want this wide and silent feeling a little more
Inside themselves.
When you go home it will seem as if your furniture
Had been waiting for you to bring it back
Its meaning,
And you won't head straight for the answering machine.
You might pour yourself a glass of iced tea
Pick up one of those snapshots framed in plastic from your table
And think about something someone told you yesterday.
Hasn't the coolness of evening arrived just a little earlier
And the angled shadows taken over just a bit more
Of the kitchen counter?
When you open your windows your rooms will smell different.
This is September
Rattling the blinds, and coming in
To touch your shoulders and the hairs on your wrists
If you have left them outside the covers
When you lie down to sleep.

THE REVIVAL OF PATSY MONTANA

It's like things I remember seeing in Seattle the lights
Of planes coming in low below the clouds that vague
Atmosphere of evening
Of gray rain delivering its sadness tonight to DC's streets
I look out the window to the alley
The rain is falling straight down and hard the owner
Of some sports car in the lot has forgotten
To close his sun roof all the way
Too bad for his leather interior
But the slick mosaic of the gravel takes this darkness
Down into the earth and will release it later
When all are sleeping soon
My father will walk into my apartment and tell me
About something terrible that happened
Twenty years ago and it will not be news
Soon the misery of this family will speak in its reluctant
Voice in some stupid Saturday night restaurant
My sister will cry
My step-mother will cradle my distant brother
Tears will make my sister's skin shine but it's not alright
Slowly the midnight will come and sooner
If I stop listening and stare at the floor
I already want to take myself down to a bar I know where
My friend the police officer will be ordering
"Vodka-in-a-glass" excitedly
As if it were an exotic drink not every bartender
Knows how to make soon the streets will look
Like smeared emotions long and dreary
And this only a week after I read that Patsy Montana
Who sang "I Wanna Be a Cowboy's Sweetheart"
Had died
Soon all the cowboys and singing cowgirls from the ancient
American night will walk into this bar I am thinking of

With their fringed pistol–belts and their guitars
And each will be identified
By their names spelled out in rope across their vests
And leather straps and I
Will have to walk over and ask them
Can you give us all a song?
And their eyes will tell me that when they finish drinking good
Then they'll begin to play

LAST BLUES

I know it's hard for you honey when you get all dressed up
And walk down U Street on your way to the bars and parties
How men call out to you from the doorways of closed
Barbeque take-outs saying
How good you look to the night
Or explaining how sorry they are
That they can't follow you home and help you hold
Your hands under your eyes so that you can cry
For one hundred hours
And I know it's hard when this is what amounts to recognition
These dirty gestures from strangers
Instead of sweet hellos from friends now that everyone
You know and love best is pregnant or dead
Or leaving for San Francisco or Carolina and I know
I too have wished for that black Cadillac
Big enough to fit all my dreams into
And long enough to take me all the way to some place
Where I might grow old and walk the beaches alone
With my pants rolled up
Watching the night come on over the world
With the dog just ahead of me
And the smell of something burning
Being carried into the darkness by the wind

Stephen Gibson was born and currently resides in our Nation's Capital. Having also lived in Boston, New York, Seattle, and San Francisco, Gibson has worked in a bookstore, at a winery, at a council for higher education, and as a bicycle messenger. The co-founder and editor of the magazine *Mobile City* recently featured on NPR's *Morning Edition*, Stephen's poems have appeared in publications like *Ploughshares* and *Poetry Northwest*. In addition, he is the author of two chapbooks, *Industrial View Facing South* and *The Waiting*.

Amidst a climate of gizmos and gadgets, dot.coms, fast food, strip malls, the ever present leaf blower and other small tragedies of 21st-century life, **Horse & Buggy Press** continues the time-honored tradition of the artisan, specifically the designer/printer. Working out of Antfarm, a co-operative studio housed in a 1925 Boylan Heights brick warehouse that originally functioned as a Carolina Washboard factory, Horse & Buggy Press integrates art, craft, literature, and design through the creation of handmade artifacts, including hand-bound letterpress printed books.

The press focuses on taking important work by contemporary writers (poets, essayists, short story writers) and publishing this work through the use of letterpress printing, handmade paper, and hand-sewn bindings in order to create important books—books that reward the reader with a true aesthetic experience in a world increasingly devoid of attention to details. Recent titles include a special illustrated edition of *It Had Wings* by Allan Gurganus, *In the Light from Stained Glass: Poems on Growing up Catholic* by Frank Ryan (named as one of the ten most outstanding books of 1999 by *Independent Publisher Magazine*), *An Elizabethan Bestiary: Retold* by Jeffery Beam (recognized as one of the 50 best books of 1998 by the AIGA), and *The Dead Father Poems*, a collaborative effort between poet John Lane and printmaker Douglas Whittle.

Please contact the press (horseandbuggypress@yahoo.com or 303 Kinsey Street, Raleigh, North Carolina 27603) if you would like to be placed on the mailing list in order to receive announcements of future books.

This first edition of *City of Midnight Skies* was designed by Dave Wofford of Horse & Buggy Press and published in three versions.

Numbers 1-250, signed and numbered, were hand-sewn and entirely letterpress printed by hand using Bembo, Craw Clarendon, Futura and Phenix types. Poem bodies were cast by Michael Bixler, all other type was hand-set by the designer/printer. Stephen's drawings were printed letterpress from engravings etched by the Brandles over on West Street. The interior paper is Everest, a 100% post-consumer recycled sheet processed chlorine-free and distributed by New Leaf Paper. The covers, handmade by Dave on Antfarm's back patio amidst the birds, the bees, the flowers and the homeless folks cutting through, were created using a myriad of plant fibers in addition to recycled matboard scraps from area frame shops.

The trade edition (500 copies) was mostly machine-printed on New Leaf Opaque, a recycled sheet processed chlorine free and distributed by New Leaf Paper (www.newleafpapcr.com): This paper contains 60% post-consumer waste content and overall is 80% recycled fiber. The covers were letterpress printed by hand.

The deluxe case-bound edition is lettered A–Z and was not only hand-printed and hand-bound, but made entirely of Horse & Buggy Press handmade paper.